T0167641

# Classic Recipes of
# HUNGARY

# *Classic Recipes of*
# HUNGARY

## TRADITIONAL FOOD AND COOKING
## IN 25 AUTHENTIC DISHES

### SILVENA JOHAN LAUTA

### LORENZ BOOKS

This edition is published by
Lorenz Books,
an imprint of Anness Publishing Ltd,
Blaby Road, Wigston, LE18 4SE

www.lorenzbooks.com;
www.annesspublishing.com

© Anness Publishing Limited 2013

If you like the images in this book and
would like to investigate using them for
publishing, promotions or advertising,
please visit our website
www.practicalpictures.com for more
information.

Publisher: Joanna Lorenz
Editor: Emma Clegg & Helen Sudell
Designer: Nigel Partridge
Production Controller: Steve Lang
Recipe Photography: Martin Brigdale

The image on the front cover is of
Hungarian Goulash, page 24

A CIP catalogue record for this book is
available from the British Library

PUBLISHER'S NOTE
Although the advice and information in this
book are believed to be accurate and true
at the time of going to press, neither the
authors nor the publisher can accept any
legal responsibility or liability for any errors
or omissions that may have been made nor
for any inaccuracies nor for any loss, harm
or injury that comes about from following
instructions or advice in this book.

PUBLISHER'S ACKNOWLEDGMENTS
The Publisher would like to thank the
following agencies for the use of their
images.Fotalia: p8bl, p9, p10bl, p11bl.
iStockphoto: p5, p6, p8t, p13.

COOK'S NOTES
Bracketed terms are intended for American
readers. For all recipes, quantities are given
in both metric and imperial measures and,
where appropriate, in standard cups and
spoons. Follow one set of measures, but
not a mixture, because they are not
interchangeable.

Standard spoon and cup measures are
level. 1 tsp = 5ml, 1 tbsp = 15ml, 1 cup =
250ml/8fl oz. Australian standard
tablespoons are 20ml. Australian readers
should use 3 tsp in place of 1 tbsp for
measuring small quantities.

American pints are 16fl oz/2 cups.
American readers should use 20fl oz/2.5
cups in place of 1 pint when measuring
liquids.

Electric oven temperatures in this book are
for conventional ovens. When using a fan
oven, the temperature will probably need to
be reduced by about 10–20°C/20–40°F.
Since ovens vary, you should check with
your manufacturer's instruction book for
guidance.

The nutritional analysis given for each
recipe is calculated per portion (i.e. serving
or item), unless otherwise stated. If the
recipe gives a range, such as Serves 4–6,
then the nutritional analysis will be for the
smaller portion size, i.e. 6 servings. The
analysis does not include optional
ingredients, such as salt added to taste.

Medium (US large) eggs are used unless
otherwise stated.

# Contents

**Introduction**                          6

Hungarian Food Culture          8

Tastes of Hungary                  10

Classic Ingredients                 12


**From the Heart of Europe 16**

Soups and Appetizers            18

Dumplings, Pasta
    and Pancakes               30

Fish Dishes                             40

Meat, Poultry and Game        44

Desserts and Bakes               54


Nutritional Notes                    63

Index                                    64

# Introduction

In the heart of Europe lies the small, land-locked country of Hungary. This flat, fertile region provides history and spectacle, from sleepy villages, baroque towns and medieval castles to the lively capital of Budapest, set in a landscape of rolling hills and a large freshwater lake. Hungary has been the homeland of many, including the Romans and the Ottoman Turks, and has seen changing fortunes as invaders from east and west, north and south arrived, leaving their own stamp on the area's agriculture and cooking. The welcoming open attitude of Hungarians has meant that their wonderfully vibrant cuisine has flourished and developed with each new change of fortune. This book celebrates this culinary diversity.

*Left: Tokay grape vineyards near the historic town of Köszeg, in Vas County.*

# Hungarian Food Culture

Hungarians have a thirst for knowledge of all kinds. Their attitude toward foreign cuisine has been to embrace and absorb new ingredients and tastes. As far back as the 9th century, the nomadic Magyar people brought recipes for hearty and wholesome stews. The Italians imported onions and garlic in the 15th century; 150 years of the Ottoman Empire saw the first use of paprika, as well as filo pastry and coffee; the

*Below: Cherry pancakes are a popular street snack.*

*Above: Fresh fruit and sour cream are the basis for many Hungarian desserts.*

Austrians passed on their love of cream, cakes and pastries; and the Germans introduced sauerkraut and dumplings.

### Hearty country fare

The cuisine of the Hungarian countryside remains much as it has been for centuries. Soups are a vital element, a filling appetizer, packed with vegetables or fruit and often topped with sour cream. Meat stews usually appear as the main course, with plenty of paprika to enliven the basic ingredients, and bread to mop up the delicious gravy. Then there will be creamy, sumptuous desserts, pies, and puddings using local fruit and nuts.

### The daily diet

The majority of Hungarians eat three good meals a day, starting with a substantial breakfast. This can include bread or pastries with butter, jam and honey, or cold sliced meat, cheese and salads of tomatoes, (bell) peppers, cucumber and radishes. Lunchtime brings the main meal of the day, and the break from work will often last as long as two hours. Soup is usually the first course, then a meat dish with pickled vegetables. Cake, strudel or sweet pancakes follow and the meal is finished with whatever fruit is in season. The evening meal tends to be a lighter affair with charcuterie and seasonal vegetables in the summer and a simple meat stew in winter.

*Right: The classic way to cook goulash is in a large pot over an open fire.*

# Tastes of Hungary

Hungary treasures its reputation as a food-lover's paradise, and much of its rich heritage has been brought in by passing traders or foreign invaders.

## The Magyar cooking pot

The nomadic tribes of ancient Hungary were always on the move making their meals in one large pot over an open fire. Dried cured beef was the base of such dishes, cooked slowly in its own juices to release all the flavour. It is still a tradition in country areas for the man of the

*Left: Dry your own peppers to make a spicy paprika mix.*

house to take charge of the large cooking pot, making a delicious beef goulash (more of a soup than a stew) for everyone to share at family occasions and celebrations.

## Paprika and coffee

Hungarian cooks gladly adapted the recipes brought to their country by Turks and Austrians from the late 16th century onwards. The warming red chilli spice paprika, so beloved of the Turks, was previously unknown in Hungary – it is now used every day in the Hungarian kitchen. There are two main forms of paprika: the delicate red one, which is added to soups and stews at the beginning of the cooking process, and the fierce orange-brown one, which is generally added at the end to give the dish an added kick. The recipes here all use sweet paprika, the more delicate form.

Coffee is another Turkish import that has become a staple of the food culture, and is said by many to have become the

*Above: Goulash is eaten throughout the year.*

national drink of Hungary. The capital Budapest in the 19th and early 20th centuries was filled with wonderfully ornate coffee houses that almost never closed and allowed the patrons to spend as much time as they liked over coffee and cake.

Hungarians tend not to drink much tea, but do enjoy a hot chocolate instead of coffee from time to time, accompanied by a rich, creamy cake in the Austrian style, or a piece of fruit strudel.

## Pasta and dumplings

Almost as important to Hungarians as it is to Italians, pasta is used as an ingredient in both savoury and sweet dishes. In the days when meat was not eaten on Fridays for religious reasons, pasta took over as the basis of a good meal with cheese or fish. There is an unwritten rule in Hungary that every dish must have its own particular shape of pasta: strawberry leaf-shaped pasta for use in soups and stews; large squares for baked meat dishes;

*Below: Dumplings feature in many Hungarian meals.*

and long, flat ribbons with sugar, lemon rind and poppy seeds as a dessert.

Dumplings are a filling favourite to accompany many stews, and can be sweet or savoury. Some are similar to Italian ravioli, while herb or plain dumplings are simmered in stock and added to the meat dish on serving.

Pancakes come in all kinds of flavours with the basic pancake wrapped around savoury or sweet variations such as feta cheese and garlic, or poppy seeds with vanilla.

*Above: Stopping for coffee and cake is a national pastime for the majority of Hungarians.*

## Pastry and cakes

Many Hungarian cake and pastry recipes were imported from Austria in the 19th century although filo pastry, the basis for the ubiquitous fruit strudel, is a Turkish speciality. Summer fruits are preserved in syrup to be used as the base for a pie in the winter months. The topping is typically made of buttery pastry enlivened with sour cream for an extra depth of richness.

# Classic Ingredients

Mention Hungarian cooking and most people will think of paprika-flavoured goulash. But there are plenty of other dishes that use all kinds of local produce, including freshwater fish, vegetables, and fruits.

### Meat, fish and game

Beef, pork and veal are the most popular meats in Hungary, and feature on every dining table in this major meat-eating country. The open plains of central Hungary are ideal for rearing beef cattle, and pigs have been raised here since Roman times. Many rural people still keep a

*Below: Rare breed Grey Longhorn cattle feed on the open plains of the Puszta.*

family pig, which is destined for hams and sausages to feed the family throughout the winter. Veal is also used, either fried simply as an escalope with a sour cream sauce, or ground to make croquettes.

People still come from all over Europe to hunt wild boar and deer in the Hungarian countryside. Venison makes a wonderful roast, and it often features as a centrepiece for family celebrations. Local people also catch hare, rabbits and pheasants, and these are cooked in delicious recipes such as fricassee of rabbit.

As Hungary has no sea coast, fresh seafish is a rarity. However, there are plenty of carp, trout, salmon, eels and pike in the rivers and lakes; these are generally cooked very simply, with a tasty sauce.

### Vegetables

The humble onion is the basic ingredient in many dishes. Chopped, it imparts flavour to goulash and pörkölt stew, or it can be left whole in soups. Until

*Above: Locally caught trout feature on many menus.*

recently, onions were sometimes eaten raw, along with bread and bacon, for breakfast in rural communities.

Hungarians love tomatoes. The word for 'tomato' and for 'paradise' is the same: paradicsom. Large tomatoes with thin skins are used for cooking, and the smaller, more decorative ones for salads. Gardeners often preserve their tomatoes for winter by making them into a mouthwatering bottled tomato sauce.

*Right: Tomatoes and onions are revered for their versatility.*

## Spices and herbs

The favourite spice of Hungary is paprika, introduced by the Ottoman Turks in the latter part of the 16th century. Paprika ranges from sweet to fiery hot, depending on the type of pepper from which it is produced. To enjoy the full flavour and aroma of paprika it should be added to hot oil, but as it burns very easily, it is best to remove the pan from the heat while adding the spice, and stir continuously. Burnt paprika tastes bitter, and will ruin a dish. Its full flavour does not last long in storage, so it is best to buy it in small quantities.

*Above: Mushrooms give earthy texture to savoury dishes.*

Mushrooms are found in the woods and fields in autumn, and the big flat ones (portobello) make an earthy base for dishes such as Transylvanian stuffed mushrooms. Smaller button mushrooms are a tasty addition to sauces and soups.

Cabbage is another staple vegetable, and one that has been cultivated for centuries. It is eaten in stews, pickled or stuffed. Many Hungarians still make their own sauerkraut, a pickled cabbage recipe brought to the country by Austrian cooks during the Austro-Hungarian empire.

*Below: Sauerkraut accompanies many cold meat recipes.*

*Above: The pungency of horseradish adds heat to a dish.*

Other strong flavours often used in Hungarian stocks or sauces are horseradish, garlic and mustard, which bring out the flavour of many a fish or meat dish. Aromatic seeds and berries such as nutmeg, caraway and juniper are used to season vegetable, fish and meat dishes by adding them to a soup stock or marinade. Poppy seeds play an important role in Hungarian cuisine, being added to many sweet cakes, breads and pancakes.

Garden herbs, such as thyme, sage, rosemary, chives, oregano, basil, tarragon and

*Above: Fresh parsley adds distinctive flavour to many dishes.*

mint also feature strongly in Hungarian cuisine. The fragrant feathery fronds of dill blends beautifully with freshwater fish such as pike, trout and salmon

*Below: Tarragon works very well with white fish.*

while parsley garnishes everything from the most delicate vegetable soup to a creamy chicken casserole.

### Dairy and eggs

Hungarians tend not to drink much fresh milk – they rarely add it to a hot drink such as tea or coffee. The dairy products they really love are sour cream and piquant cheeses such as feta cheese, goat's cheese, quark (curd cheese) and, above all, cottage cheese. Sour cream is often used for thickening sauces and soups, or adding to the much-loved Hungarian paprika-flavoured chicken dish, papricas.

Cottage cheese makes a delicious dip when blended with the ubiquitous paprika, or as a simple topping for dumplings and pancakes. Hungarian cheeses tend to be pale, soft and sharp, such as feta or ricotta, or the more solid Trappista, a traditional semi-soft cheese originally made in the monasteries of France from the 17th century.

*Above: Feta cheese is added to salads or to stuff mushrooms.*

Eggs are often served hard-boiled and sliced as part of a buffet salad, or finely chopped in mayonnaise dressing. They are also key in the cooking of cakes.

*Below: Rural families keep chickens for their fresh eggs.*

# From the Heart of Europe

This small country nestling in the centre of Europe is rightly proud of its culinary traditions. Throughout the years of foreign domination, whether by Mongols, Turks, Austrians or Russians, Hungarians have preserved their favourite dishes and passed them down from one generation to the next. The generosity of spirit of the Magyar people, the original Hungarian tribe, spills over into the size of their meals and no visitor is allowed to go home hungry. Hungarian cooks have merged these many influences with their own local produce to create a lasting legacy of richly nourishing food. The recipes that follow celebrate this fine heritage.

*Left: Hungarians' love of wholesome food is evident in their home cooking and in their restaurants.*

# Morello Cherry Soup
## Hideg meggyleves

**Serves 6**

700g/1¾lb morello or sour cherries, stoned
1.5ml/¼ tsp mixed (apple pie) spice
juice and grated rind (zest) of 1 lemon
1 litre/1¾ pints water
75ml/5 tbsp caster (superfine) sugar
1 large egg yolk
250ml/8fl oz/1 cup sour cream
6–7 mint sprigs, leaves only, to serve
10ml/2 tbsp ground pistachios, to serve

**COOK'S TIP**
For maximum flavour use cherries that have a bright, shiny and firm (but not hard) flesh. The darker the flesh, the sweeter the taste.

*Soups made from seasonal fruits are a favourite central European treat, and cherry soup is one of the glories of the Hungarian table. It is delicious served with an extra spoonful or two of sour cream.*

**1** Trim the cherries and wash them. Place in a pan with the mixed spice, lemon juice and rind. Cover with the water and add the sugar.

**2** Bring to simmer and cook for 10 minutes. Remove half of the cherries, using a slotted spoon. Use a food processor to process the mixture until you get a smooth purée. Return to the soup and bring to boil.

**3** Place the egg yolk and sour cream in a bowl and mix to combine. Add a cup of the cherry soup into the egg mixture and stir to mix well. Return the mixture to the rest of the soup.

**4** Allow to simmer very gently for 2–3 minutes and remove from heat. Serve with mint and pistachios on top.

# Chilled Gooseberry Soup with Blackberries
## Hideg egresleves szederrel

**Serves 6**

450g/1lb/4 cups gooseberries,
  trimmed
60ml/4 tbsp caster (superfine) sugar
juice and grated rind (zest) of 1 small
  lemon
100ml/3½fl oz/½ cup sweet white
  wine
15ml/1 tbsp cornflour (cornstarch)
60ml/4 tbsp sour cream
a handful of blackberries, to serve

*This cooling summer soup is made with sweet wine and fresh gooseberries, which are a valuable source of fibre and vitamins A and C. As well as being a tasty appetizer, the soup can also be paired with boiled meat or meat patties as a main meal. If you can get hold of the sweet, aromatic wine, Tokay, then this soup is just amazing.*

**1** Put the gooseberries in a large pan with the sugar. Add the lemon rind and juice with 1 litre/1¾ pints/4 cups water and the wine. Bring to the boil over medium heat and simmer for 20–25 minutes, or until the gooseberries are soft.

**2** In a small bowl, mix the cornflour with the sour cream until smooth. Gradually add about 200ml/7floz/ scant 1 cup of the hot cooking liquid, stirring to make a smooth and creamy consistency.

**3** Stir into the gooseberry mixture in the pan and mix well to combine. Cook for 2 minutes, then cool and chill completely before serving. Serve cold, topped with fresh blackberries.

# Cream of Cabbage and Horseradish Soup
## Tormás káposztakrémleves

**Serves 6**

30g/1¼oz/2½ tbsp butter
1 onion, finely chopped
675g/1½lb Savoy cabbage, finely shredded
5ml/1 tsp caraway seeds
1.5 litres/2½ pints/6¼ cups chicken stock
30ml/2 tbsp plain (all-purpose) flour
15ml/1 tbsp creamed horseradish
30ml/2 tbsp crème fraîche
115g/4oz/1¼ cups freshly grated Parmesan cheese
salt and ground black pepper

**1** Melt 10g/¼oz/½ tbsp butter in a large pan and add the onion. Fry gently for 1 minute, then add the cabbage. Stir well and add the caraway seeds. Pour in the chicken stock and then cook for around 10–15 minutes.

**2** Meanwhile, make a roux by heating the remaining butter in a small frying pan and adding the flour. Stir the roux until smooth then cook, gradually adding some of the hot stock from the soup to combine with the roux.

**3** Add the roux mixture to the pan with the soup. Stir well to combine and season with salt and pepper. Add the horseradish and stir well. Cook for 15 minutes more.

**4** Remove from the heat and blend the soup in a food processor or blender until smooth. Return to the pan and add the crème fraîche. Serve the soup hot, topped with Parmesan cheese.

*This is a perfect combination: smooth and creamy Savoy cabbage with a hint of horseradish. Hungarians use freshly grated horseradish root, but this recipe is a little milder and uses creamed horseradish instead.*

# Mushroom and Tarragon Soup
## Tárkonyos gombaleves

**Serves 6**

300g/11oz field (portobello)
  mushrooms
30ml/2 tbsp olive oil
2 shallots, finely chopped
600ml/1 pint/2½ cups vegetable
  stock
30ml/2 tbsp chopped fresh tarragon,
  plus extra leaves, to garnish
45ml/3 tbsp sour cream
salt and ground black pepper
crusty bread, to serve

*This delightful combination
of ingredients sees the
earthy flavours of the
mushrooms combine with
the sour cream and fresh
tarragon to produce a
satisfying and warming
appetizer or main meal.*

**1** Clean and slice the mushrooms quite finely.

**2** Add the olive oil to a large pan and heat gently. Add shallots, sauté
for 2–3 minutes and add the mushrooms. Sauté for 5 minutes.

**3** Add the stock and season. Simmer for 15–20 minutes, covered.

**4** When the soup has thickened, add the tarragon and remove the soup
from the heat.

**5** Add the sour cream and mix to combine, while the soup is still hot.
Serve, garnished with tarragon, and accompanied with crusty bread.

# Squash Soup with Chestnuts
## Gesztenyés sütőtökleves

**Serves 6**

1.2kg/2½lb summer squash
(courgettes (zucchini), yellow
crookneck squash, and scallop
squash), with skin and seeds
removed and flesh cut into
squares
60–90ml/4–6 tbsp olive oil
4 shallots, finely chopped
30ml/2 tbsp cognac
115g/4oz/1 cup of chestnuts,
skinned and chopped
200ml/7fl oz/1 cup sour cream
200ml/7fl oz/1 cup vegetable stock
5ml/1 tsp finely chopped marjoram
5ml/1 tsp finely chopped fresh sage
115g/4oz/1 cup shelled pecan nuts,
toasted and coarsely chopped
salt and ground black pepper

*Chestnuts are used in
Hungarian dishes
throughout the year, either
fresh or preserved. Use
summer squash as they
have tender flesh that needs
a minimum of cooking.*

**1** Preheat the oven to 190°C/375°F/Gas 5. Put the squash in a roasting pan, coat with 45ml/3 tbsp olive oil, and bake in the oven for 1 hour. Cool and place the soft flesh into a small container.

**2** In a pan, heat the remaining oil and fry the shallots gently until soft. Add the cognac and simmer over low heat until almost all the liquid has evaporated. Add the chestnuts and fry for 3 minutes.

**3** Add the squash to the pan and remove from the heat, mixing well. Put the mixture in a food processor or blender and purée until soft, adding some sour cream and vegetable stock to help the blending.

**4** Return the soup to the pan, and add more sour cream and stock to achieve the desired consistency. Season with salt and pepper. Cook over low heat for 10–15 minutes. Finally, add the herbs. Serve the soup hot, sprinkled with the pecan nuts and garnished with marjoram.

# Hungarian Goulash Gulyásleves

**1** Heat the oil in a heavy pan or flameproof casserole dish over medium heat and gently fry the onion until soft without browning. When the onion turns transparent, add the beef and stir to sauté the meat with the onions. Add the garlic and caraway seeds.

**2** Take the pan or casserole off the heat and add the paprika (see Cook's Tip), stirring constantly to make sure that the paprika is absorbed well by the meat. Add 1.5 litres/2½ pints/6¼ cups water and simmer gently for at least 1 hour.

**3** Check that the meat is cooked by testing a small piece. If you are happy with it, add the tomatoes, green pepper and potatoes. Otherwise, cook for about 20 minutes longer before you add the vegetables. Season to taste and simmer for a further 30 minutes.

**4** For an authentic combination, serve hot accompanied by galuska, the dumplings that are traditionally served with goulash.

### COOK'S TIP
Paprika is never added over direct heat.The pan must be removed from the heat to add the paprika, because paprika has a high sugar content; if added directly over the heat it would burn and become bitter in taste.

*Here is the traditional recipe for this hearty dish, named after the herdsmen (gulyás) who prepared the meal in a cast-iron kettle over an open fire as they were working in the pasture. In the West we tend to eat goulash as a stew, but Hungarian goulash is a thin soup with plenty of meat and vegetables. It can be prepared in advance and is therefore ideal to use for a party or family gathering. Two ingredients are of utmost importance: paprika and caraway.*

## Serves 6
45ml/3 tbsp vegetable oil
1 large onion, chopped
800g/1¾lb good-quality stewing
  beef, cut into 2.5cm/1in cubes
1 garlic clove, crushed
2.5ml/½ tsp caraway seeds
30ml/2 tbsp sweet paprika
2 tomatoes, chopped
1 green (bell) pepper, seeded and
  thinly sliced
300g/11oz potatoes, peeled and
  cubed
salt and ground black pepper
Hungarian dumplings, to serve (see
  pages 32–33)

# Transylvanian Stuffed Mushrooms
## Erdélyi töltött gombafejek

**Serves 4**

300g/11oz/4½ cups mushrooms
oil, for greasing
185g/6½oz smoked bacon, cut into
   small cubes
250g/9oz/generous 1 cup ricotta
   cheese
8 thyme sprigs, leaves finely chopped
salt and ground black pepper
green mixed leaf salad, to serve

**1** Preheat the oven to 180°C/350°F/ Gas 4. Remove the stems from the mushrooms and reserve for another dish. Arrange the mushrooms on a greased baking tray.

**2** Cook the bacon in a non-stick pan over medium-high heat until golden brown. Remove the bacon and put in a bowl to cool. Season with salt and pepper.

**3** Add the ricotta cheese and thyme. Mix well to combine. Spoon into the prepared mushrooms, piling on the filling.

**4** Cook the stuffed mushrooms in the oven for 10–12 minutes, or until the tops are melting and golden. Remove and serve with crisp green salad leaves.

**COOK'S TIP**
Clean the mushrooms before preparation by wiping each one with a damp cloth.

*This dish is usually served with creamy polenta or cornmeal, the staple ingredients of the Transylvanian shepherds' diet. Because of this frequent pairing of ingredients, this dish is also known as 'shepherd's mushrooms'. Ricotta cheese is used here, but home-made cottage cheese would have been a traditional choice.*

# Cottage Cheese and Sweet Paprika Dip
## Körözött

**Serves 4**

300g/11oz/scant 1½ cups túró curd (farmer's) cheese or cottage cheese

115g/4oz/½ cup cream cheese

1 small bunch of spring onions (scallions), finely chopped

30ml/2 tbsp sour cream

15ml/1 tbsp sweet paprika

30ml/2 tbsp caraway seeds

2.5ml/½ tsp mustard powder

1 garlic clove, crushed

small bunch of chives, finely chopped

salt and ground black pepper

toasted crusty bread, to serve

*Paprika is the star ingredient of this spicy dip and makes a frequent appearance in other dips from the region. Sweet paprika is often combined with yogurt, cream cheese or mayonnaise, but here we have a low-fat variation with cottage cheese.*

**1** Combine the túró curd cheese or cottage cheese and cream cheese in a bowl and season to taste with a little salt and ground black pepper.

**2** Add the chopped spring onions, sour cream, paprika, caraway seeds, mustard powder, garlic and fresh chives. Stir together well, then serve with toasted crusty bread.

**VARIATION**

You can prepare this recipe only with cream cheese if you want a smoother texture and are not worried about the extra calories.

**SERVING IDEAS**

This ideal party dip can be served with chicken pieces and crudités such as green beans, cherry tomatoes and cucumber and carrot sticks.

# Pike and Horseradish Pâté
## Tormás csukapástétom

**Serves 6**

200g/7oz fresh pike fillets, bones
    removed
50g/2oz/4 tbsp butter, softened
15ml/1 tbsp creamed horseradish
    (or horseradish sauce below)
5ml/1 tsp sour cream
a pinch of caster (superfine) sugar
2 small eating apples
ground black pepper

**For the horseradish sauce**

45ml/3 tbsp grated fresh horseradish
15ml/1 tbsp white wine vinegar
10ml/2 tsp caster (superfine) sugar
150ml/¼ pint/⅔ cup double (heavy)
    cream

**To serve**

rye bread, sliced red onion, apple
    rings, sour cream and parsley

*Pike has lean, firm, bony
flesh and a delicate flavour,
and tastes wonderful when
combined with pungent
horseradish and sour cream.*

**1** To make the horseradish sauce, put the horseradish, vinegar and sugar into a bowl and mix well. Whip the cream until it is thickened and fold in the horseradish mixture. Cover and chill the sauce.

**2** Chop the pike fillets into pieces and put in a food processor or blender with the butter, creamed horseradish, sour cream, sugar and black pepper to taste.

**3** Pulse the fish and the horseradish sauce until it is smooth but not minced (ground).

**4** Peel the apples and grate finely, adding them to the fish mixture. Mix well and chill until ready to use.

**5** To serve, spread the pâté on to the rye bread, and top with the onion and apple rings. Finish with some sour cream and a sprig of parsley.

# Herb Semolina Dumplings in Chicken Soup
## Fűszeres daragaluska tyúkhúsleves

### Serves 6

60ml/4 tbsp butter, melted
2 eggs
6 dill sprigs, finely chopped
6 thyme sprigs, leaves finely chopped
6 parsley sprigs, leaves finely chopped
200g/7oz/generous 1 cup semolina
1 litre/1¾ pints/4 cups chicken stock

### For the soup

225g/8oz chicken breast fillets
oil, for frying
1 onion, sliced
1 medium carrot, sliced
1.2 litres/2 pints/5 cups chicken stock

**1** To make the soup, chop the chicken fillets into 2.5cm/1in cubes. Heat the oil in a large pan, add the chicken, onion and carrot and cook, stirring, until the meat is browned all over. Add the stock, bring to the boil and then lightly simmer for 20 minutes until the chicken and vegetables are cooked through. Set aside and keep warm.

**2** To make the dumplings, put the butter and eggs in a bowl and whisk until fluffy. Add the herbs and semolina and mix well.

**3** Heat the chicken stock in a large pan to boiling point. Using a teaspoon, scoop off small amounts of the semolina mix to form the dumplings and drop them into the boiling stock.

**4** Cook until the dumplings have risen to the top, and have become plump and fluffy.

**5** Remove with a slotted spoon, add to the chicken soup and serve.

### COOK'S TIPS

• Use coarse semolina, because finely ground semolina will create a denser dumpling that will cook more slowly.
• The dumplings can be made a few hours ahead of the meal – just cover them lightly with clear film (plastic wrap) so they don't dry out. Alternatively, they can be frozen until needed.

*These small semolina dumplings are perfect for soups, particularly a clear chicken broth. The herbs make them attractive as well as adding flavour. The light and fluffy little balls are delicate and tantalizing as they float on the soup.*

# Hungarian Dumplings Galuska (nokedli)

**1** Beat the eggs with 5ml/1 tsp salt and 200ml/7fl oz/scant 1 cup water. Add a little flour to make a smooth and thick mixture, then add the remaining flour and beat with a wooden spoon until the dough is glossy and exceptionally smooth.

**2** Add the herbs and mix in well. Adjust the dough with more flour, if necessary, until it comes away from the sides of the bowl.

**3** Place the dough on a board and, using a teaspoon, cut off pieces about 2.5cm/1in long and to the thickness of a pencil. Add the noodles to a pot of boiling water. Alternatively, push the dough through a dumpling strainer directly into the boiling water.

**4** Cook until the galuska rise to the top of the water, then drain them in a colander.

**5** Sauté the cubed bacon in a non-stick pan with the vegetable oil until golden and crispy. Serve the hot galuska as a light meal with some melted butter and topped with crispy bacon. Alternatively, serve with a soup or stew.

**Serves 6**

2 eggs
about 300g/11oz/2⅔ cups plain (all-purpose) flour
45ml/3 tbsp finely chopped fresh mixed herbs, such as parsley, tarragon, thyme and rosemary
200g/7oz bacon, cubed finely
30ml/2 tbsp vegetable oil
salt
melted butter, to serve

*The most famous dumplings in Hungary, galuska are a traditional accompaniment to all porkölt dishes (the national paprika stew). Galuska are also commonly offered when serving goulash and soups. They can be made from different kinds of dough and are always small. One of the most memorable galuska taste experiences is served at the world-famous Gundel restaurant in Budapest.*

# Poppy Seed Pasta with Goat's Cheese
## Mákos metélt kecskesajttal

**Serves 4**

400g/14oz/3½ cups plain (all-purpose) flour
3 eggs
pinch of salt
115g/4oz/1 cup poppy seeds
grated rind (zest) of 1 orange
60ml/4 tbsp butter, melted
30ml/2 tbsp caster (superfine) sugar
30ml/2 tbsp honey
150g/5oz goat's cheese, crumbled

**1** Sift the flour into a bowl and make a well in the middle. Add the eggs and salt. Mix roughly, then gradually add 200–300ml/7fl oz–½ pint/scant 1–1¼ cups water. Keep mixing until you have a soft and workable dough.

**2** Knead for 10 minutes, then put the dough in a bowl, cover with a dish towel and allow to rest for 15 minutes.

**3** Roll the dough as thinly as you can, using either a pasta machine or a rolling pin. This may take some time – the dough needs to be paper-thin. Cut into shapes of your choice, perhaps long, thin strips or rectangles or triangles. Traditionally, this recipe would have made long, thin noodles.

**4** Bring a large pan of water to the boil and drop in the home-made pasta. Cook for just 2–3 minutes, until just tender. Drain and keep warm.

**5** Add the poppy seeds, orange rind, butter and sugar. Toss to combine. Serve, drizzled with honey and topped with goat's cheese.

*This is best prepared using a pasta machine, so that you can make exceptionally thin layers. If a machine is not available, roll out the pastry as thinly as you can. Here it is dressed with a Hungarian favourite, poppy seeds, as well as butter, orange, honey and goat's cheese.*

# Pinched Noodles
## Csipetke

**Serves 4**

130g/4½oz/generous 1 cup plain
    (all-purpose) flour
1.5ml/¼ tsp salt
1 egg
30ml/2 tbsp water
15ml/1 tbsp melted butter
fried bacon and sour cream
    (optional), to serve

*Something between a noodle and a dumpling, csipetke are served to accompany soups or stews. They are best cooked separately and then added to the dish, but they can also be served with bacon and sour cream as an accompaniment.*

**1** Put the flour, salt and egg in a bowl. Stir to combine and make a dough. Add a little water and knead until the dough is smooth and free from lumps. Wrap in clear film (plastic wrap) and chill for 30 minutes.

**2** When ready to cook, remove from the refrigerator and allow to stand for 10 minutes. Roll to a 5mm/¼in thickness and then pinch pieces off, roughly 2cm/¾in in size.

**3** Have a large pan of boiling water ready and drop the dough pieces in, a few at a time. Cook until they are soft and have risen to the top, about 10–12 minutes.

**4** Remove with a slotted spoon and toss in the melted butter. Either serve the dumplings on their own, accompanied by fried bacon and sour cream, or add to a soup or stew just before serving.

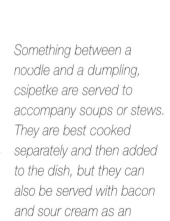

# Pancake and Wild Mushroom Stacks
## Gombás rakott palacsinta

**Serves 8**

15ml/1 tbsp butter, melted
500g/1¼lb/8 cups wild mushrooms,
　cleaned and roughly chopped
2 eggs
100ml/3½fl oz/scant ½ cup sour
　cream
115g/4oz/½ cup cream cheese
3–4 tarragon sprigs, chopped
8–10 pancakes (for method, see
　pancake recipe on page 38)
melted butter, for brushing
115g/4oz/1 cup grated Cheddar
　cheese
salt and ground black pepper

*Stacks of filled pancakes
are very common in
Hungary and are often
prepared for a special
dinner party. It is an
easy dish to prepare and
you can pre-cook the
pancakes well in advance,
then assemble them at the
last minute with your filling.*

**1** Preheat the oven to 180°C/350°F/ Gas 4. Heat the butter in a non-stick pan and add the mushrooms. Sauté for 5–7 minutes, or until soft, and season to taste. Discard any cooking liquid.

**2** Meanwhile, beat the eggs with the sour cream and cream cheese, and season to taste. Stir into the cooked mushroom mixture with the chopped tarragon.

**3** Arrange a pancake in a greased round cake tin (pan). Spread on a layer of the mushroom mixture, then top with another pancake. Continue in this way until all the pancakes and filling have been used, finishing with a pancake.

**4** Brush with butter and sprinkle with the grated cheese. Bake for 30 minutes, or until golden brown. Serve in wedges, with salad leaves.

# Pancakes with Creamy Feta Cheese and Wild Garlic Sajtos-fokhagymás palacsinta

**Serves 4**

200g/7oz/1¾ cups plain (all-purpose) flour
2 eggs
250ml/8fl oz/1 cup milk
100ml/3½fl oz/scant ½ cup soda water
60–75ml/4–5 tbsp clarified butter, or olive oil, canola oil or another vegetable oil, if preferred

**For the filling**

250g/9oz feta cheese, crumbed
15ml/1 tbsp thick natural (plain) yogurt
100ml/3½fl oz/scant ½ cup sour cream
115g/4oz/4 cups wild garlic leaves, finely chopped
salt and ground black pepper

**VARIATION**
For a lighter version, substitute the feta cheese with cottage cheese.

**1** Put the flour, eggs and milk in a large bowl and whisk to make a smooth batter. Gradually add the soda water to make a slightly thinner consistency, similar to double (heavy) cream.

**2** To make the filling, put the feta cheese in a bowl, then add the yogurt, sour cream and wild garlic. Season to taste and mix well to combine.

**3** Heat some of the clarified butter or oil in a non-stick frying pan and add a small ladleful of the pancake batter. Tilt the pan so that the batter covers the base of the pan and cook for 1 minute on each side, or until golden and crisp. Lift the edge with a palette knife or metal spatula to see if it is tinged gold before turning. Use the remaining batter to make eight to ten pancakes.

**4** Spread some of the cheese, yogurt and sour cream filling in a thin layer over each pancake. Roll each one up and serve.

**COOK'S TIPS**
• It is advisable to start with a small amount of batter, and then slowly add more batter in the pan if you want to increase the pancake size.
• If you are not sure exactly when to turn the pancake, then pay attention to the bubbles forming and then popping around the edges. When these bubbles pop and the hole does not close up immediately, then the pancake is ready to be turned over.

*Here is a classic pancake recipe that can be adapted for any menu, and can be served with sweet or savoury fillings. Hungarians use soda water in their pancake mixture to make the pancakes light and fluffy. If you can't find wild garlic, fresh herbs will also taste wonderful with the feta cheese.*

# Light Hungarian Fish Stew Halászlé

**Serves 4**

1kg/2¼lb mixed fresh fish (carp, perch, eel, trout or other freshwater fish)
2 large onions, roughly chopped
15ml/1 tbsp medium hot paprika
1 red (bell) pepper, cubed
1 tomato, chopped
salt and ground black pepper
white bread, to serve

**1** Remove the head and bones from the fish and wash them. Cut the flesh into small pieces and set aside.

**2** Put the fish heads and large bones in a large pan with the onions and cover with water. Season with salt and pepper, add the paprika and bring the mixture to the boil. Simmer gently for 1 hour.

**3** Strain the stock and discard the solids, then return the stock to the rinsed pan and add the prepared pepper, tomato and fish.

**4** Cook over low heat for 20 minutes. Serve with fresh white bread.

**COOK'S TIPS**
• Combining different freshwater fish will increase the soup's aromatic quality.
• For a fish stew it is advisable to use at least a medium-hot paprika. The accompanying bread is designed to cool the fire of the paprika.

*Fish stews and soups would traditionally have been prepared in small kettles on an open fire, mostly by fishermen themselves. These dishes, prepared with a mixture of river fish, offered a nutritious and comforting peasant meal. Every part of Hungary has its own recipe.*

# Hungarian Cod Casserole Tepsis tonhal

**Serves 4**

20g/¾oz/½ tbsp butter, for greasing
800g/1¾lb baby new potatoes,
    peeled and sliced
800g/1¾lb cod fillets, cut into
    chunky pieces
2 bunches of spring onions
    (scallions), finely chopped
200ml/7fl oz/scant 1 cup sour cream
2.5ml/½ tsp sweet paprika
salt
green salad (optional), to serve

*The majority of fish used in Hungarian dishes will have been fished from the Danube and Tisza Rivers. While cod is not a freshwater fish and would have been sourced from a coastal fishing port, it did feature on the traditional Hungarian table in a chunky oven-baked casserole.*

**1** Preheat the oven to 150°C/300°F/ Gas 2. Butter an oval ovenproof dish and arrange the sliced potatoes over the base, and season with salt. Put the pieces of fish on top.

**2** Arrange the spring onions on top of the fish. Pour the sour cream over and sprinkle with the paprika.

**3** Bake for 40 minutes. Serve with a green salad, if liked.

# Salmon with Whipped Yogurt Sauce
## Lazac joghurtmártással

**Serves 4**

4 salmon fillets, about 300g/11oz
  each
30ml/2 tbsp flour
45ml/3 tbsp olive oil
4 egg whites
2 egg yolks
200ml/7fl oz/scant 1 cup thick
  natural (plain) yogurt
small bunch of dill, finely chopped
salt and ground black pepper
green salad, to serve

**1** Preheat the oven to 160°C/325°F/ Gas 3. Dust the salmon fillets in the flour and season with salt and pepper.

**2** Heat the olive oil in a non-stick frying pan. Sauté the salmon for 2 minutes on each side, or until cooked through. Remove and arrange in a flat ovenproof dish.

**3** Put the egg whites into a clean, grease-free bowl and whisk for a few minutes, until foamy.

**4** Put the egg yolks and yogurt in another bowl and mix to combine, then season to taste with salt and pepper. Add the dill.

**5** Fold the egg whites into the egg yolk mixture and pour over the salmon. Bake for 10 minutes. Serve with a green salad.

**VARIATION**
The recipe can also be prepared with smoked haddock or cod.

*The savoury, earthy and slightly sweet taste of salmon is universally appreciated. Whether farmed or wild, salmon are elegant to look at, light to eat, reliably tasty and a healthy food choice, being one of the richest sources of beneficial Omega-3 fats. This dish is simple to prepare, sautéed then baked and served to perfection with a creamy and cleansing yogurt-based sauce.*

# Chicken and Paprika Stew with Sour Cream
## Paprikás-tejfölös csirkepörkölt

**1** Heat the oil in a heavy pan and cook the onion until just golden. Remove from the heat and add the paprika, stirring well.

**2** Return the pan to the heat and add the chicken, 50ml/2fl oz/¼ cup water and the tomatoes. Season with salt and pepper, mix well, then cover and cook for 15 minutes, adding a little more water if necessary.

**3** Remove the lid and continue cooking over low heat for 15 minutes more. Add the sliced green peppers and stir well.

**4** Combine two-thirds of the sour cream with the flour, if using, and add to the sauce.

**5** Cook over a low heat for 5–7 minutes, then serve the stew with a dollop of the remaining sour cream.

### COOK'S TIPS
• Paprika, as with other spices that have been ground, will lose its potency over time, so aim to use it within six months.
• When buying paprika, choose a tin container rather than a glass bottle because light will damage the spice.
• Store paprika in an airtight container in a cool, dark place, ideally the refrigerator.

*Papricas, pronounced 'papricash', is another traditional stew typical of Hungary. It is always made with lean meat – veal, chicken or rabbit – and cooked with sour cream. It is likely to become a family favourite at mealtimes, and this recipe is well tried and tested, prepared in homes and restaurants since the end of the 18th century.*

**Serves 6**
45ml/3 tbsp vegetable oil
1 onion, chopped
5ml/1 tsp sweet paprika
4 large skinless chicken breast fillets, cut into 2.5cm/1in cubes
2 large tomatoes, cubed
2 green (bell) peppers, seeded and thinly sliced
300ml/½ pint/1¼ cups sour cream
10ml/2 tsp plain (all-purpose) flour
salt and ground black pepper

**Serves 4**

2 slices white bread
100ml/3½fl oz/scant ½ cup milk
500g/1¼lb/5 cups veal, minced
  (ground)
75ml/5 tbsp finely chopped fresh
  parsley
1 large egg
vegetable oil, for shallow frying
200g/7oz/3½ cups brioche
  breadcrumbs
salt and ground black pepper
tomato and onion salad, to serve

**For the stuffing**

30ml/2 tbsp of vegetable oil
1 small onion, finely chopped
115g/4oz/1 cup walnuts, chopped
115g/4oz/scant 1 cup raisins
1.5ml/¼ tsp ground cumin
1.5ml/¼ tsp ground cinnamon

# Veal Croquettes Borjúfasírt

**1** Preheat the oven to 180°C/350°F/Gas 4. Soak the bread in the milk for 5 minutes. Gently squeeze out the excess milk, and break the bread into small pieces.

**2** Put the bread into a medium bowl, add the veal mince, parsley and egg, and season with salt and pepper. Mix well to combine.

**3** To make the stuffing, heat the oil in a large frying pan and sauté the onion for 3 minutes. Add the walnuts and allow them to gently brown, then add the raisins, cumin and cinnamon, and cook gently for another 5 minutes. Remove from the heat.

**4** Take a small handful of the veal mixture and form into a flat disc. Put a tablespoonful of the walnut stuffing in the centre and wrap the edges around it, rolling it into a largish meatball. Gently form an oval croquette. Repeat with the remaining veal mixture and stuffing.

**5** Put the oil for shallow frying into a frying pan. Roll the croquettes in the brioche crumbs and fry gently for 3 minutes on each side to brown. Transfer to an ovenproof dish and cook in the oven for 15 minutes. Serve hot, with a tomato and onion salad.

**COOK'S TIP**
• Mini-croquettes can also be fun, in which case, mould smaller shapes from the veal mixture.
• When you fry the croquettes, ensure that they are not touching and keep rolling them in the oil.

*These mouthwatering croquettes provide a tasty light lunch or a more substantial evening meal. The walnuts and raisins give a layered texture to the stuffing of the veal discs, which are then quickly fried before developing a crusty shell during a short spell in the oven.*

# Hussar Beef
## Marhaszelet huszár módra

**1** Melt the butter in a large, heavy non-stick pan over low heat and add the onion. Add the paprika and the bacon and cook for 5 minutes.

**2** Add the green peppers, mushrooms, tomato and peas. Season to taste and add the veal stock. Cook over high heat for 5 minutes, then reduce to a simmer for another 10 minutes, or until the liquid has almost evaporated.

**3** Pour the oil into a non-stick frying pan and add the beef. Season with salt and pepper, and cook for 4–5 minutes on each side for medium. Serve the beef fillet accompanied by the cooked vegetable mixture and boiled rice.

### COOK'S TIP
Beef tenderloin is the roast cut from the centre of the tenderloin – it is best eaten with a pink centre. Over-cooking a beef fillet will make it dry and tasteless.

### VARIATION
Use lamb or chicken for a lighter option.

**Serves 4**

50g/2oz/4 tbsp butter
1 onion, chopped
5ml/1 tsp sweet paprika
115g/4oz smoked bacon, cubed
2 green (bell) peppers, chopped
200g/7oz/2¾ cups wild mushrooms, sliced
1 tomato, chopped
150g/5oz/1½ cups peas
100ml/3½fl oz/scant ½ cup veal stock
15ml/1 tbsp olive oil
4 fillet steaks (beef tenderloins) (200g/7oz each)
salt and ground black pepper
rice, to serve

*Fillet of beef is associated with a lack of visible fat and a tender texture. This name refers to the Hussars, who rode with cuts of beef beneath their saddles to tenderize them.*

# Venison Meatballs
## Szarvas-húsgombóc

**1** Put the venison and veal in a bowl with the onion, and season with salt and pepper.

**2** Add the breadcrumbs, oregano and egg to the bowl, and mix them well to combine.

**3** Shape the meat mixture into meatballs and dust with the flour.

**4** Fry the meatballs in the olive oil over medium heat for 12–15 minutes, turning to cook evenly. Remove and keep warm.

**5** Off the heat, add the paprika to the pan, followed by the chicken stock. Bring to the boil, then simmer until reduced by half.

**6** Add the sour cream and fresh herbs. Pour over the meatballs and serve on warmed plates.

**Serves 4**

400g/14oz/4 cups coarsely minced (ground) venison
200g/7oz/2 cups minced (ground) veal
1 onion, finely chopped
45ml/3 tbsp breadcrumbs
5–6 oregano sprigs, finely chopped
1 egg, beaten
5ml/3 tbsp plain (all-purpose) flour, for dusting
60ml/4 tbsp olive oil
2.5ml/½ tsp sweet paprika
100ml/3½fl oz/scant ½ cup chicken stock
45ml/3 tbsp sour cream
a handful of fresh herbs, leaves chopped
salt and ground black pepper

*After preparing an initial meal of venison, any unused pieces can be minced (ground) to make delicious meatballs, served in a sour cream sauce. You can use other meats, perhaps wild boar, beef or veal.*

# Fricassée of Rabbit and Prunes
## Nyúlbecsinált szilvával

**1** Preheat the oven to 160°C/325°F/Gas 3. In a heavy flameproof casserole, brown the onion in the olive oil, then add the leeks, carrots and celery, and sauté for 5 minutes.

**2** Arrange the rabbit pieces over the vegetables, then pour in the wine and chicken stock. Add the cloves, parsley and bay leaves, and season with salt and pepper.

**3** Put the casserole in the oven and cook for 1½ hours, or until the rabbit is tender. Take out of the oven and keep warm. Pour out the cooking liquid and keep it in reserve.

**4** In a shallow pan, melt the butter, then add the flour and cook until light brown. Gradually add most of the cooking liquid, stirring until the sauce is thick and smooth. Mix the egg yolks and cream together in a bowl and add them to the sauce. Simmer gently – do not allow it to boil.

**5** Add the thyme and prunes to the sauce, then pour into the casserole dish with the rabbit. Return to the heat and simmer for 2–3 minutes, then serve with plain boiled rice.

*While not among the core ingredients used in the Hungarian kitchen, many people like this distinctive meat that is high in protein and lower in cholesterol and fat than chicken, beef or pork. This fricassée throws a mélange of flavourful vegetables, along with eggs and cream, into the mix, with the unexpectedly delightful final addition of prunes.*

**Serves 4**

1 onion, chopped
30ml/2 tbsp olive oil
2 leeks, white part only, sliced
2 carrots, sliced
2 celery sticks, sliced
2 rabbits, chopped into portions
100ml/3½fl oz/scant ½ cup dry white wine
300ml/½ pint/1¼ cups chicken stock
10 cloves
2 parsley sprigs
5 fresh bay leaves
50g/2oz/4 tbsp butter
30ml/2 tbsp plain (all-purpose) flour
3 egg yolks
120ml/4fl oz/½ cup single (light) cream
30ml/2 tbsp chopped fresh thyme leaves
115g/4oz/½ cup prunes, stoned (pitted) and sliced
salt and ground black pepper
rice, to serve

# Rice and Almond Pudding
## Habos-mandulás rizsfelfújt

**Serves 6**

200g/7oz/1 cup pudding rice
400ml/14fl oz/1⅔ cups double
  (heavy) cream
750ml/1¼ pints/3 cups full-fat
  (whole) milk
150g/5oz/¾ cup caster (superfine)
  sugar
15ml/1 tbsp almond extract
3 egg whites
45ml/3 tbsp flaked (sliced) almonds,
  lightly toasted

**1** Preheat the oven to 180°C/350°F/ Gas 4. Put the rice and two-thirds of the cream into a heavy pan, and cook over medium heat for 2–3 minutes.

**2** Mix well and then add the milk and 30ml/2 tbsp of the sugar. Cook on low heat for another 10–15 minutes, or until the rice grains are soft. When the liquid has more or less evaporated, add the remaining cream and the almond extract.

**3** Spoon the egg whites into a clean, grease-free bowl and whisk until they form soft peaks. Whisk in the remaining sugar to make a light meringue.

**4** Pour the rice pudding into six individual ovenproof dishes, and either pipe the meringue mixture on top of each pudding, using a piping bag, or just spoon the mixture over.

**5** Sprinkle the tops with the almonds. Cook for 8–10 minutes, or until the tops of the meringues are slightly golden in colour.

*This is an adaptation of a traditional Hungarian recipe. It is a textural delight, containing the creamy comfort of rice pudding, the luxury of golden meringue tops and the occasional crunchy encounter with toasted almonds, all in all a show-stopping dessert.*

# Hungarian Cherry Strudel
## Cseresznyés rétes

**1** Preheat the oven to 200°C/400°F/Gas 6. Butter a baking sheet and line with baking parchment. Put the cherries and lemon juice in a pan and cook over medium heat for 2 minutes.

**2** In a large bowl, mix together the apples, walnuts, sugar and breadcrumbs. Stir in the cherries. Put the cherry jam in a pan and heat gently until melted.

**3** Lay out a damp cloth on the work surface and put a sheet of filo pastry on top (cover the remaining pastry sheets with a damp cloth to stop them from drying out). Brush generously with melted butter, then cover with another sheet of filo, brushing again with butter.

**4** Repeat with another sheet of filo pastry, but this time also brush it with melted cherry jam. Repeat the same process with the remaining filo sheets, brushing every third sheet with the cherry jam.

**5** Once you have all the filo buttered and stacked in front of you, put the apple, cherry and walnut mixture in the middle of it and roll the pastry up as though it were a Swiss roll (jelly roll).

**6** Brush butter over all the sides of the roll, then put on to the prepared tray, seam-side down, with the pastry edge beneath the roll. Sprinkle over some caster sugar and curl into a horseshoe shape. Bake in the preheated oven for 20–30 minutes, until golden brown. Leave to cool on a wire rack.

**Serves 8**

750g/1lb 10oz fresh cherries, pitted
65g/2½oz/5 tbsp butter, melted, plus
    extra for greasing
15ml/1 tbsp lemon juice
3 cooking apples, cored, peeled and
    cut into segments
70g/2¾oz/generous ½ cup walnuts,
    roughly chopped
75g/3oz/6 tbsp caster (superfine)
    sugar, plus extra for sprinkling
30g/1oz/½ cup brioche breadcrumbs
60ml/4 tbsp cherry jam
10 large sheets fresh filo pastry,
    thawed if frozen
caster (superfine) sugar, to sprinkle

**COOK'S TIP**

It is best to make strudel on a warm day, because the dough can be rolled more easily in a hot room.

*Making strudel pastry can be time-consuming, although in the countryside, Hungarian women still make their own – and there's nothing like the real thing. A true strudel should be fine, crisp and light, with very thin pastry filled with fruit.*

# Raspberry and Almond Gratin
## Málnás-mandulás szelet

**Serves 6**

10ml/2 tsp butter, melted, for
    greasing
115g/4oz/1 cup pistachio nuts, finely
    chopped
50g/2oz/⅔ cup brioche breadcrumbs
50g/2oz/¼ cup soft light brown
    sugar
5ml/1 tsp vanilla extract
150ml/¼ pint/⅔ cup double (heavy)
    cream
2 large eggs
500g/1¼lb/3⅓ cups raspberries,
    washed
thick natural (plain) yogurt, to serve

**1** Preheat the oven to 200°C/400°F/ Gas 6 and lightly butter a 20cm (8in) medium square cake tin (pan).

**2** Put the pistachio nuts, brioche crumbs, sugar, vanilla, cream and eggs in a food processor and blend them until combined. (Alternatively, beat the eggs, then add in the other ingredients and stir well.)

**3** Spread out the raspberries in one layer over the base of the cake tin. Pour in the gratin mixture. Bake for 30 minutes.

**4** Leave for 5 minutes to cool in the tin, then turn out and serve warm, accompanied by thick natural yogurt.

**VARIATION**
Raspberries make a successful taste pairing with various other fruits – including blueberries, blackberries, or figs. Just add any one of these fruits in combination with the raspberries over the base of the cake tin.

*This recipe is from Carmel Pince, possibly the best Jewish restaurant in Budapest. The dish can also be prepared with cherries. The use of pistachio nuts is an ancient Ottoman influence in Hungarian cooking.*

# Poppy Seed Pastries with Cottage Cheese
## Túrós-mákos csomagok

**Makes 20**
oil, for greasing
250g/9oz/generous 1 cup cottage
   cheese
200g/7oz/scant 1 cup curd (farmer's)
   cheese
5ml/1 tsp ground black pepper
1 large egg yolk
20 sheets filo pastry, thawed if frozen
150g/5oz/10 tbsp butter, melted
30ml/2 tbsp poppy seeds
75–90ml/5–6 tbsp clear honey

*The Hungarians like
contrasts in their food, and
the combination of salty and
sweet is as common as the
flavours of sweet and sour.
The salty–sweet partnership
works best by using creamy
home-made cottage
cheese, which in this recipe
is combined with the natural
sweetness of honey.*

**1** Preheat the oven to 180°C/350°F/ Gas 4 and grease a baking sheet. Combine the cottage cheese and curd cheese in a bowl, then stir in the black pepper and egg yolk.

**2** Take a sheet of filo pastry and cover the remaining pastry sheets with a damp cloth. Lightly brush the sheet of filo with some melted butter and fold in half lengthways. Brush with butter and fold it in half again.

**3** Put some cheese mixture on the pastry along the shorter edge and roll the pastry over the filling away from you to form a small Swiss roll (jelly roll). Make sure you fold the sides of the pastry inward at the same time, to enclose the filling. Do not roll too tightly. Put on to the baking sheet. Continue with the remaining filo sheets and cheese mixture.

**4** Brush the pastries with melted butter, then sprinkle with poppy seeds. Bake in the oven for 20 minutes, or until golden brown. Serve warm with a little honey to drizzle over the pastry.

# Hungarian Chocolate Almond Torte
## Mandulás csokoládétorta

**Serves 10–12**

150g/5oz/10 tbsp butter, plus extra
    for greasing
200g/7oz dark (bittersweet)
    chocolate (containing 70% cocoa
    solids), chopped
6 large eggs, separated
150g/5oz/⅔ cup soft light brown
    sugar
30ml/2 tbsp plain (all-purpose) flour
115g/4oz/1 cup ground almonds

**For the ganache**

150ml/¼ pint/⅔ cup double (heavy)
    cream
200g/7oz dark (bittersweet)
    chocolate (containing 70% cocoa
    solids), chopped

**For the almond topping**

150g/5oz/¾ cup caster (superfine)
    sugar
200g/7oz/1¾ cups flaked (sliced)
    almonds, roasted

**1** Preheat the oven to 180°C/350°F/Gas 4. Grease and line a 20cm/8in round cake tin (pan), and line it with baking parchment. Melt the butter over low heat. Remove from the heat and add the chopped chocolate, stirring constantly so that it melts in the hot butter. Leave to cool.

**2** In a large bowl, whisk the egg yolks and sugar together until thick and pale. Add the chocolate mixture and mix well. Sift in the flour and ground almonds, and carefully mix together.

**3** Put the egg whites into a clean, grease-free bowl and whisk until they form soft peaks. Fold the egg whites carefully into the mixture to retain as much air as possible in the batter. Pour into the prepared tin and bake for 25 minutes. The cake will be set but slightly wobbly in the centre. Leave to cool in the tin.

**4** To make the ganache, heat the cream to almost boiling point. Immediately remove from the heat and add the chopped chocolate. Stir until all of it is amalgamated. Cool and then pour over the cake to glaze. Leave to set.

**5** To make the almond topping, lightly oil a sheet of baking parchment. Put the sugar and 100ml/3½fl oz/scant ½ cup water in a pan and cook until lightly caramelized. Remove from the heat and add the flaked almonds. Stir briefly to coat.

**6** Using tongs, and working quickly, take out small clusters of the sticky nuts and put on the baking parchment to cool. Top the cake with the almond clusters and serve.

*This cake is inspired by the rich and delectable tortes served in the little Café Ruszwurm in Budapest, which is easily the best place to have classic Hungarian cakes and pastries.*

# Hungarian Christmas Loaf Beigli

### Serves 8

300g/11oz shortcrust pastry, thawed
  if frozen
flour, for dusting
1 egg yolk, beaten
15ml/1 tbsp icing (confectioners')
  sugar, to serve

### For the walnut filling

300g/11oz/2¾ cups walnuts, roughly
  chopped
200g/7oz/1 cup caster (superfine)
  sugar
75ml/5 tbsp single (light) cream
1.5ml/¼ tsp ground cinnamon
45ml/3 tbsp raisins
10ml/2 tsp vanilla extract
grated rind (zest) of 1 lemon
15ml/1 tbsp orange marmalade

*This is a loaf that every
Hungarian family will prepare
for the Christmas
celebrations. It is a little like
a strudel but is instead
made with shortcrust pastry.
Walnuts and dried fruits are
always used for the filling.*

**1** Preheat the oven to 180°C/350°F/ Gas 4 and line a baking sheet with baking parchment. To make the walnut filling, put the chopped walnuts and sugar into a bowl and mix together well.

**2** Put the cream and the walnut mixture into a pan and cook over medium heat until it becomes the consistency of a thick purée. Remove from the heat. Add the cinnamon, raisins, vanilla extract, lemon rind and marmalade and mix.

**3** Roll out the pastry on a floured board to a large rectangle about 3mm/⅛in thick. Spread the walnut filling over the rectangle, leaving a border of 1cm/½in around the edges.

**4** Roll up the dough sheet, starting from the longer side, then lay it seam-side down on the baking sheet. Brush with the egg yolk and bake for 15–20 minutes, or until golden brown. Cool completely and sprinkle with icing sugar before serving.

# Nutritional notes

**Morello Cherry Soup**: Energy 212kcal/889kJ; Protein 3g; Carbohydrate 28g, of which sugars 28g; Fat 10g, of which saturates 6g; Cholesterol 62mg; Calcium 63mg; Fibre 1.8g; Sodium 30mg

**Chilled Gooseberry Soup with Blackberries**: Energy 118kcal/499kJ; Protein 1g; Carbohydrate 22g, of which sugars 20g; Fat 2g, of which saturates 1g; Cholesterol 6mg; Calcium 33mg; Fibre 3.2g; Sodium 9mg

**Cream of Cabbage and Horseradish Soup**: Energy 202kcal/841kJ; Protein 11g; Carbohydrate 11g, of which sugars 6g; Fat 13g, of which saturates 8g; Cholesterol 24mg; Calcium 278mg; Fibre 4g; Sodium 663mg

**Mushroom and Tarragon Soup**: Energy 329kcal/1356kJ; Protein 1g; Carbohydrate 5g, of which sugars 15g; Fat 35g, of which saturates 6g; Cholesterol 5mg; Calcium 15mg; Fibre 1.3g; Sodium 268mg

**Squash Soup with Chestnuts**: Energy 392/1621kJ; Protein 5g; Carbohydrate 16g, of which sugars 9g; Fat 34g, of which saturates 7g; Cholesterol 20mg; Calcium 98mg; Fibre 3.7g; Sodium 182mg

**Hungarian Goulash**: Energy 320kcal/1336kJ; Protein 31g; Carbohydrate 14g, of which sugars 4g; Fat 16g, of which saturates 4g; Cholesterol 84mg; Calcium 29mg; Fibre 2.3g; Sodium 160mg

**Transylvanian Stuffed Mushrooms**: Energy 244kcal/1012kJ; Protein 16g; Carbohydrate 2g, of which sugars 1g; Fat 19g, of which saturates 8g; Cholesterol 61mg; Calcium 160mg; Fibre 1.7g; Sodium 825

**Cottage Cheese and Sweet Paprika Dip**: Energy 237kcal/984kJ; Protein 12g; Carbohydrate 6g, of which sugars 5g; Fat 19g, of which saturates 11g; Cholesterol 44mg; Calcium 193mg; Fibre 0.8g; Sodium 418mg

**Pike and Horseradish Pâté**: Energy 220kcal/921kJ; Protein 9g; Carbohydrate 23g, of which sugars 11g; Fat 11g, of which saturates 6g; Cholesterol 40mg; Calcium 48mg; Fibre 2.9g; Sodium 324mg

**Herb Semolina Dumplings**: Energy 227/953kJ; Protein 7g; Carbohydrate 26g, of which sugars 0g; Fat 11g, of which saturates 6g; Cholesterol 99mg; Calcium 24mg; Fibre 1.3g; Sodium 486mg

**Hungarian Dumplings**: Energy 337kcal/1514kJ; Protein 13g; Carbohydrate 39g, of which sugars 1g; Fat 16g, of which saturates 5g; Cholesterol 102mg; Calcium 99mg; Fibre 2.4g; Sodium 626mg

**Poppy Seed Pasta with Goat's Cheese**: Energy 691kcal/2905kJ; Protein 29g; Carbohydrate 92g, of which sugars 16g; Fat 42g, of which saturates 18g; Cholesterol 241mg; Calcium 675mg; Fibre 3.6g; Sodium 489mg

**Pinched Noodles**: Energy 161kcal/679kJ; Protein 5g; Carbohydrate 25g, of which sugars 1g; Fat 5g, of which saturates 2g; Cholesterol 66mg; Calcium 55mg; Fibre 1.2g; Sodium 168mg

**Pancake and Wild Mushroom Stacks**: Energy 318kcal/1325kJ; Protein 11g; Carbohydrate 22g, of which sugars 1g; Fat 21g, of which saturates 12g; Cholesterol 162mg; Calcium 179mg; Fibre 2.3g; Sodium 226mg

**Pancakes with Creamy Feta Cheese and Wild Garlic**: Energy 598kcal/2493kJ; Protein 22g; Carbohydrate 48g, of which sugars 6g; Fat 37g, of which saturates 22g; Cholesterol 216mg; Calcium 464mg; Fibre 2.8g; Sodium 1211mg

**Light Hungarian Fish Stew**: Energy 432kcal/1809kJ; Protein 48g; Carbohydrate 13g, of which sugars 10g; Fat 21g, of which saturates 5g; Cholesterol 271mg; Calcium 85mg; Fibre 2.8g; Sodium 274mg

**Hungarian Cod Casserole**: Energy 350kcal/1476kJ; Protein 41g; Carbohydrate 34g, of which sugars 4g; Fat 6g, of which saturates 3g; Cholesterol 103mg; Calcium 51mg; Fibre 2.6g; Sodium 2274mg

**Salmon with Whipped Yogurt Sauce**: Energy 749kcal/3118kJ; Protein 69g; Carbohydrate 10g, of which sugars 4g; Fat 49g, of which saturates 9g; Cholesterol 256mg; Calcium 191mg; Fibre 90.3g; Sodium 339mg

**Chicken and Paprika Stew with Sour Cream**: Energy 309kcal/1288kJ; Protein 27g; Carbohydrate 8g, of which sugars 6g; Fat 19g, of which saturates 8g; Cholesterol 100mg; Calcium 69mg; Fibre 2.1g; Sodium 154mg

**Veal Croquettes**: Energy 518kcal/2158kJ; Protein

13g; Carbohydrate 39g, of which sugars 5g; Fat 36g, of which saturates 5g; Cholesterol 67mg; Calcium 161mg; Fibre 2.4g; Sodium 490mg

**Hussar Beef**: Energy 539kcal/2249kJ; Protein 52g; Carbohydrate 10g, of which sugars 0g; Fat33g, of which saturates 15g; Cholesterol 168mg; Calcium 46mg; Fibre 6.1g; Sodium 732mg

**Venison Meatballs**: Energy 383kcal/1608kJ; Protein 38g; Carbohydrate 21g, of which sugars 3g; Fat 18g, of which saturates 5g; Cholesterol 146mg; Calcium 79mg; Fibre 1.9g; Sodium 351mg

**Fricassée of Rabbit and Prunes**: Energy 588kcal/2452kJ; Protein 44g; Carbohydrate 24g, of which sugars 17g; Fat 34g, of which saturates 15g; Cholesterol 341mg; Calcium 174mg; Fibre 6.9g; Sodium 302mg

**Rice and Almond Pudding**: Energy 668kcal/2786kJ; Protein 10g; Carbohydrate 62g, of which sugars 33g; Fat 44g, of which saturates 26g; Cholesterol 109mg; Calcium 197mg; Fibre 1.4g; Sodium 103mg

**Hungarian Cherry Strudel**: Energy 343kcal/1443kJ; Protein 17g; Carbohydrate 44g, of which sugars 38g; Fat 14g, of which saturates 5g; Cholesterol 17mg; Calcium 51mg; Fibre 5.0g; Sodium 147mg

**Raspberry and Almond Gratin**: Energy 282kcal/1179kJ; Protein 9g; Carbohydrate 20g, of which sugars 14g; Fat 19g, of which saturates 6g; Cholesterol 100mg; Calcium 75mg; Fibre 6.1g; Sodium 213mg

**Poppy Seed Pastries with Cottage Cheese**: Energy 101kcal/428kJ; Protein 15g; Carbohydrate 8g, of which sugars 6g; Fat 3g, of which saturates 1g; Cholesterol 15mg; Calcium 63mg; Fibre 0.5g; Sodium 118mg

**Hungarian Chocolate Almond Torte**: Energy 636kcal/2653kJ; Protein 12g; Carbohydrate 51g, of which sugars 48g; Fat 45g, of which saturates 18g; Cholesterol 176mg; Calcium 113mg; Fibre 3.5g; Sodium 135mg

**Hungarian Christmas Loaf**: Energy 584kcal/2437kJ; Protein 9g; Carbohydrate 54g, of which sugars 36g; Fat 39g, of which saturates 7g; Cholesterol 36mg; Calcium 87mg; Fibre 5.2g; Sodium 191mg

# Index

beef
  Hungarian goulash 24
  Hussar beef 49

cabbage and horseradish soup,
  cream of 20
cherry strudel, Hungarian 56
chicken and paprika stew with
  sour cream 45
chocolate almond torte,
  Hungarian 60
Christmas loaf, Hungarian 62
cod casserole, Hungarian 41
coffee 10
cottage cheese and sweet
  paprika dip 28

dumplings 11
  herb semolina dumplings with
    chicken soup 30
  Hungarian dumplings 33

fish
  Hungarian cod casserole 41
  light Hungarian fish stew 40
  pike and horseradish pâté 29
  salmon with whipped yogurt
    sauce 42

fruit
  chilled gooseberry soup with
    blackberries 19
  Hungarian cherry strudel 56
  Morello cherry soup 19
  raspberry and almond gratin 58

gooseberry soup with
  blackberries, chilled 19
goulash, Hungarian 10, 24

herb semolina dumplings, 30
Hungarian ingredients 12–15
Hussar beef 49

Morello cherry soup 18
mushrooms
  mushroom and tarragon soup
    22
  pancake and wild mushroom
    stacks 37
  Transylvanian stuffed
    mushrooms 26

noodles, pinched 36

pancakes
  pancake and wild mushroom
    stacks 37
  pancakes with creamy feta
    cheese and wild garlic 38
paprika 10
paprika dip, sweet, and cottage
  cheese 28
pasta 11
  poppy seed pasta with goat's
    cheese 34

pike and horseradish pâté 29
poppy seed pasta with goat's
  cheese 34
poppy seed pastries with cottage
  cheese 59

rabbit and prunes, fricassée of 53
raspberry and almond gratin 58
rice and almond pudding 54

salmon with whipped yogurt
  sauce 42
soup
  chicken soup, with herb
    semolina dumplings 30
  chilled gooseberry soup with
    blackberries 19
  cream of cabbage and
    horseradish soup 20
  Morello cherry soup 18
  mushroom and tarragon soup
    22
  squash soup with chestnuts 23
strudel, Hungarian cherry 56

veal croquettes 46
venison meatballs 50

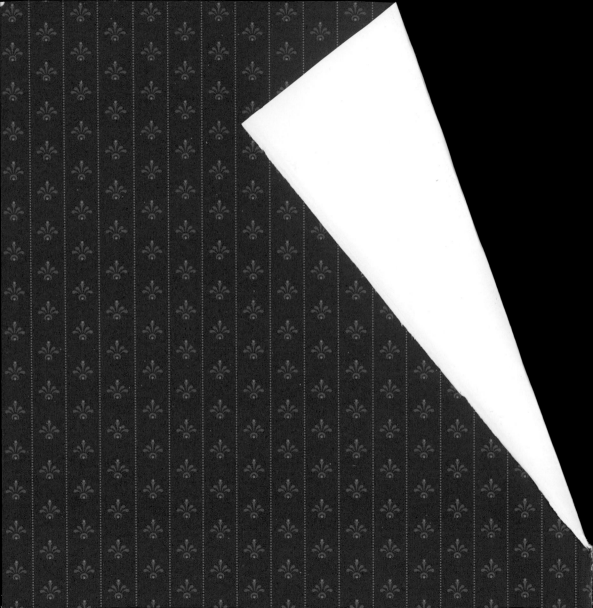